Out to See

by

Marilyn Kendall

DORRANCE PUBLISHING CO., INC.
PITTSBURGH, PENNSYLVANIA 15222

Dorrance Publishing Co., Inc.
701 Smithfield Street
Pittsburgh, PA 15222
Visit our website at *www.dorrancebookstore.com*

ISBN: 978-1-4349-1833-8
eISBN: 978-1-4349-1753-9

T hank you, Hunter, for the encouragement you gave to me to share this story and giving me the confidence to do so. I suppose everyone can gather enough material from their journey to weave the thread into the garment of their life of many colors. We all have a story, and there are many places in which one can say, "Been there, done that." We are similar and yet different. The journey is a continual roller coaster of ups and downs, climbing small hills, to mountaintop experiences, and coming down the other side into dark valleys of the unknown. Sometimes the best way over a mountain is through it, not around it or over it.

Keep an open mind, and attach yourself to nothing.

I was born into a life of privilege and British heritage. My mother married late in life and my father was even later, being twenty years older. I knew little about my father's family, and family matters were never discussed. Mother, on the other hand, made sure we understood our roots, class structure, and where we came from. Perhaps this was one reason she was so determined to drum it into us.

The story begins in pre-WWII in Manchester, England. Class structure and position in society was the way of life. Family was bound tightly and socialization was within the confines of family. It was a grand life. We lived in a large house and spent happy times with family. Sunday afternoons were spent at the seaside with open symphony on the pier. I was the first-born child. My father worked as a merchant accountant for a large firm. He was a brilliant man and natural with figures. Father was a short, stout little man with a big round belly that shook when he laughed like a bowl full of jelly. He was, however, far from a Father Christmas. He engaged little with the family and was a regular at the local pub. Most social gatherings were done in the local pubs. He was a good provider, although Mother always felt the class structure and felt she married below her station.

Mother was a large woman with big breasts that met the table long before her body. She was obviously a wonderful cook. She could clean a crab like no other. We always had fresh organic food long before the push to eat the natural food we have today. There was little disease and our diet consisted of real butter, cream, and lots of sweets. A trip to the local shops was done on a daily basis. There were no supermarkets but rather stores specific to what was sold, e.g., meat, produce, bakery, and fish. Being first-born Mother was overprotective and strong.

My maternal grandmother was a dear, sweet woman and very partial to me as her first grandchild. We established a strong, special bond. She would make bread and save the end for me. At one time she even wanted me to come live with her, but Mother of course put her foot down as she oh so often did. I guess you practice on the firstborn and lighten up as additional children come along.

Mother's uncle was a court magistrate and wore the white wig and long black robe. My uncle and his wife were quite old when they had their two daughters. They lived in a country manor on top of a hill. Many of my growing years were spent at the manor. Mother used to love to sit on the toilet looking out the window over the moors. It was a grand place with a long staircase we would slide down. There were large oil paintings hanging on the walls of our family's ancestors. My aunt and uncle were the most important family members in the village, and I was proud to be part of that family dynamic.

When I was ten, another child, my sister, Scarlett, was added to the family, then came my brother several years later. By the time my brother got to my age, just about anything he wanted to do was acceptable. Maybe Mother and Dad were simply too old and worn out to do battle. It is usually easier to say yes than no even when no should be said. I remember one time a family portrait was being taken, and it was my job as the eldest to keep brother clean in his little white suit. Of course, being all boy, he got on the floor and got dirty. I was in trouble. There were lots of long faces in that picture except, of course, baby brother smiling from ear to ear.

We had a wonderful big house in Manchester, and we spent our holidays at the manor house. I used to bathe with my two younger cousins until my old aunt told Mother that due to my rapidly developing body, I was no longer allowed to continue that activity. As a young girl moving toward puberty and womanhood, I was crushed when Mother delivered the news. All these things were happening to me physically, but mentally I was still a child.

There were fewer and fewer visits to my happy place. Family dynamics were rapidly changing. As Father got older, the world was changing. When his employer of many years realized he was not a Catholic, Father lost his job. WWII was fast approaching. There was little work, and what jobs were available were not possible for Father at his age and he was overlooked.

WWII was declared and the bombing started. The streets were dark and the raids began. It was frightening. The government was threatening to take the children out of the country, separating families. Mother was desperate. I was grown and wanted to join the military, but Mother put a stop to that. I had a good friend who wanted me to move to London, but I was denied. I wanted to work in the local bakery, but Mother said I was above that menial job.

Big decisions had to be made in a brief time. Mother looked for a home to move the family to. Unknown at that time was that Hitler kept that city safe for his potential playground. The only place available was a small row house near the sea. We packed up and moved inland to that tiny place: Mother, Father, myself, sister, and brother. The bedrooms were the size of a closet, and it was a stark contrast to our big house in Manchester, which by the time we moved was bombed, so the decision to move was confirmed or it would have been the end of the story. We moved from a free-standing house with many rooms to a small semi-detached bungalow.

Father was unemployed and never got another job. He started drinking more and stayed out of the house most of the time. He was very bigoted and didn't like Catholics, Jews, or blacks. Father was cranky and I didn't get along with him on any level. I never had much respect for him and was embarrassed to bring friends home. I never considered this little place my home. I would refer to the big house we had left in the city as my home. There was a lot of story to come before the end of my life journey. The upside of the move for me was that my dear grandmother lived in this village. I wanted to live with her but was denied as always. I would run to her frequently for tea and the first slice of homemade bread she always saved for me. She made me feel special, and I thought I could tell her anything.

By the time the move was made, I was out of school and looking for work. All the British men were sent overseas, leaving the American GI's. I was fortunate enough to get an office job for the government. The air raids were becoming more frequent, and you could tell by the sound of the planes which ones were the German ones. They had a different sound.

All the young adults hung out at the two dance halls. There was live organ music, lots of GI's, and good times. My sister, Scarlett, and I would dress up and go out to make new friends. Scarlett was a beautiful girl with curly raven hair and long legs. I always thought she was the pretty one. We had to share a space and she would drive me crazy. Scarlett was messy and took my things without asking, returning them often stained or damaged. I begged Mother for a space of my own. She said the only place would have to be in the attic. I was willing to accept anything as an alternative to where I was.

I worked hard to fix my space when I wasn't working and was happy to move on up when it was completed. The anticipation and excitement was brief after I spent my first night. Being near the sea, you could hear the winds combined with the rains and sirens. The messy space with Scarlett didn't seem so bad. I never complained again.

When we returned from a night out, she would often drop me in favor of the company of a GI who turned her head. I was forced to return home alone. It was frightening, as I would run down the road in complete darkness when the lights were all extinguished during the raids. I often ran in darkness hoping to remember where all the turns were. Mother did her best to establish a normal home, but nothing about it was normal or the memories I cherished. My sister and brother were young enough not to know or remember how life had been. It was good for them but made me sad and bitter. It made me sad for my dear mother, as her lifestyle was so different from what her roots were.

She was reduced yet again to an even lower standard. She tried to instill the values and class she had in her children.

The gathering places for young adults were at two large dance halls in the city. They were grand places with a large ballroom and an organ that came up from the floor. The music was always performed by a live orchestra, and the songs were as timeless today as they were then. We would go there to meet and greet old and new friends. There were more new friends than old, as the British men were shipped to Europe to fight the war, leaving the American soldiers as our new friends. The base was not far from the city, and it was loaded with lonely men far from home, looking for a friend or good time.

Although Scarlett and I were several years apart, the years seemed to get shorter as we aged and we were best friends. When we would go out, she would go from one guy to another. I was much more grounded and preferred to get to know the fellows I met. I was a stable one-guy type of girl. We would line the walls waiting to be asked for a dance. I think my prince was born dancing. One tall, dark, and handsome American GI in particular caught Scarlett's eye, but after one drink and one dance she turned her back on him and moved to another. He struck up a conversation and we talked and talked. We clicked and soon became friends. It was a fireworks-earth-moving moment. He was dashing in his uniform; tall, dark, and handsome defined him. He was charming and sweet. He was different from anyone I had ever met. I felt like Cinderella who met her prince. My heart would skip a beat at the very mention of his name, John. I was dizzy in love.

John was smitten with me and wanted to meet my family. I put him off over and over, not wanting him to see where or how I lived. We began meeting on a regular basis, but instead of dancing we would sneak off to the seaside. My awakened hormones, along with his, were in sync. We would kiss and fondle among the rock alcoves by the sea for hours. John was determined and finally, after explaining my living situation, it was clear he loved me for me and nothing else seemed to matter.

The lady in the flat next to ours rented rooms to generate income, so when John would come to visit he would rent a room from her and spend the night. In addition to the need to be near me, it was a break from the military job he had. When John entered the military, he wanted to train to be a pilot but he was too tall. John was placed in the mechanical area. His main responsibility was to clean the planes that returned from battle, often containing blood, body parts, and wounded and dead soldiers.

Mother took a liking to him from the first moment. John was charming and didn't know a stranger. It was a fair distance from the base, but he would make it to my home as often as he could. It seemed as if the war would never end, and I knew I was in love with this tall, dark, handsome fellow. I attempted to break the relationship. My American was such a salesman. After work, when I would come home, I would find him sitting at the kitchen table with Mother. John received cigarette rations, but since he was a non-smoker he sold them to Mother. They were fast friends.

Father was depressed, as he was unable to find work, and spent a majority of his time in the local pubs. Father and I got along like oil and water. He never engaged with me or my sister or brother.

As time went by, my American was told he would be returning to the States. I had a myriad of emotions. John adored me and soon shared the dark secret he carried. John was actually married, had a son, and was recently divorced. Seems he had slept with the town tramp in the small Midwest farm town back home. John and every other male, including his brothers. She pointed at him as the father of the boy, and he did the honorable thing; he married her and assumed responsibility for the child. John left soon after and never saw the child. The marriage was a mistake, and they divorced. The court told John he must fulfill his financial obligation and pay her $25 a month in child support.

By the time John shared the news, I was deeply in love and could not imagine my life without him. John said the divorce was final and asked me to marry him. He called me his English rose. I could not imagine how my life and journey would unfold.

John and I approached Mother with the news, asking for a blessing. Mother was confused and had mixed emotions. How could this happen, and how could she let her beloved first-born go? On the flip side, there were no men and I was a young woman in love, ready to be a wife. At this time and age, Mother knew she no longer had control or could make decisions for me. Mother liked my choice for a soulmate but certainly not the prospect of losing me to the other side of the world. I had great respect for her, but love overruled any concerns for Mother's feelings. I was ready to be a wife, I was ready to establish my own life, and I wanted to run far away from where I was. I wanted to fly. I was ready to go to the next level in our relationship. I had never been with a man and knew nothing. I just knew I was ready to have that experience.

I had a best friend, and she and her husband traveled to a nearby village with us for the nuptials. There was no big wedding, cake, or dress. My family didn't even come. I wore a suit and he was in uniform. It was simple and quick. We had a meal with my friend and her husband and then traveled to the south of England for a few nights. We could only find a small hotel on the seaside and book the room. There were many firsts, including an encounter with bedbugs. My first night and sexual encounter was everything and more than I had daydreamed about. John knew how to meet my needs, and I felt the earth move. It was magical and we were inseparable.

We had found a small flat in the village not far from the base. Playing house as a new bride was brief, and the days flew by all too soon. When we returned to my village and the military base, John was greeted with orders to return to the States. Although we were married, it was complicated to immigrate to the States. Some if not most decisions are made for you, and John left for the other side of the world.

Being alone in a room of people took on a new meaning as the reality of separation, void, and loneliness nestled in. Never let weakness convince you that you lack strength. My family tried to fill the void to no avail. My very soul had been awakened, and there was only one person in the whole world who could fill that void.

There were hundreds of war brides in the same situation, and the paperwork was backlogged. John had no choice but to leave me with my family with a promise to have me join him as soon as it could be done. The war was still raging with no end in sight. I was left in the small flat with my family as a married woman with raging hormones. I ached for John and was lonely and depressed, waiting day after day at the mailbox for some information about going to the States to be reunited with my husband or get mail from him confirming his love for me. That always lifted my spirits, but I still felt empty and lonely. It was never enough. My days and nights seemed to run together.

My father even attempted to life my spirits, but his breath smelled of alcohol, and a relationship that had been strained for years could not be mended in a short time. Food was rationed and Mother tried her best to care for her family. The family was faced with food rationing. My father would keep special cookies in his drawer to share; however, the special treat was tainted with the smell and taste of mothballs from the drawer he hid them in. We dared not say a word; we were thankful and ate the special treat with a happy heart. Although I had little in common with Father, I always had great respect for him, as God's commandment had been to honor thy mother and father.

I felt worse than ever. Here I was, a married woman trapped in a small flat with what seemed like no end in sight. My flighty sister, Scarlett, encouraged me to go to the dance hall with her one night to help lift my spirits. I wasn't much company but agreed to go to just get out of the house to a different environment and bring back memories of happy times. Scarlett was dancing with all the men as usual, and I sat quietly at a table daydreaming when I was approached by yet another charming American soldier. He sat next to me and we began to talk. We talked for hours, and I imagined it was my tall, dark, handsome husband, John. Alas, it was not, but a girl can dream. It was smoky and noisy, so we went outside for some air. I thought it was harmless and agreed. The closeness of the dance and unsatisfied needs awakened my physical need to be with a man. I remembered the tender touch and smell and excitement of the physical experience.

The nameless, faceless soldier took my hand. I thought my heart would jump from my chest. Every emotion I had felt with my John came flooding in. I think I would have slept with any man who would have me. I still had the flat I shared with John before he left, so I invited my new friend in for more than a goodnight kiss. Anything looks the same in the dark, and I imagined it was my tall, dark, handsome husband and could actually imagine looking into his dark eyes. Alas, John was on the other side of the world, and I was so lonely and bitter to have been left behind. We had a wild night of sex. It was not my prince, but it was sex and I didn't seem to care.

At morning light, the soldier slipped away into the morning light, thanking me for the good time. I never saw him again. I felt dirty and ashamed. Should I have even asked to be paid for the good time like a prostitute?

As time passed, it seemed an eternity. Reality soon kicked in, and I was overwhelmed with a sense of shame. To me he was nameless and faceless and yet reminiscent of my glorious brief married days. I knew I had sinned but accepted blame for my decision. How could I let the weakness of the flesh allow me to lower my standards and compromise my vows and fidelity to John? I thought about how I had let this happen in the very bed I shared with John. I had even broken one of God's commandments. I vowed right then and there it would never happen again and hoped somewhere along the line I would be granted forgiveness. I never shared my fall from grace, but that wasn't my decision.

I slipped into a deeper depression and was so ashamed of my adulteress encounter. I justified it as just another casualty of war. My papers were still being processed, and I kept looking at the mail to be notified that I could travel to the new world to be with John. Alas, one day ran into another. My life was just a succession of days going back and forth from my government office job. At times the streets would go dark and you could hear the fighter planes going over. You knew from the sounds if it was American or German aircraft, as the German planes had a particular high-pitch sound. I was so afraid and would run home in fear, wondering if I would make it. I kept thinking of my fall from grace and wondered what fate I would have from my sin. I felt sick most of the time, from guilt, poor nutrition, or just longing for John.

Money was tight and I moved back home, living in the tiny bungalow with my family. The walls seemed to get closer and closer, and I would close my eyes at night and imagine life in the big house I was born into and my happy place. As my health continued to deteriorate, I decided I needed to see a physician for some kind of relief. I made the appointment and went after work one day. After some consultation and exam, the doctor informed me I was with child.

A flood of emotions and scenarios brought me to my knees. I explained to the staff that my husband was an American and was shipped back to the States. I was waiting for my papers to be able to make the journey across the pond to join him. Yet another lie was born, as I made them believe the child I carried was from my husband when in fact it was a bastard child conceived in sin. As I had no money, it was suggested I hire the services of a midwife and prepare for a home birth.

I left the office armed with a stack of information and confusion. I walked home, slowly playing out different ways to reveal this news, knowing I had a small window. A baby is supposed to be a blessed event; however, I knew I was to carry a child formed from an adulteress act. What was I to do and what was I to say? How was I to tell? Yet I knew I had a timeline to make all that happen. For a brief moment, I just wanted to die, but I knew God had put life in me and I had a responsibility to carry that gift. How could I go home? The impending birth of a child could not be kept secret for long. I had to face reality and take whatever punishment God had in store for me. I knew I had to deal with it quickly. I really had a sinking feeling and had to pause to be ill before I made it home. My chin was on the ground, along with my spirit. I remember Mother always told me many things could be taken away but no one could kill your spirit. I knew I had to dig deep now, as a new life was preparing to come into the world and I was the carrier for it.

I pondered the thought of a baby and was lifted with the notion that I would have something of my own to love and nurture regardless of the consequences. I had to be honest for the first time in my life. I was an honest person and never lied, but this was a big one. I had to come clean and tell the truth.

By the time I got home, Father was at the local pub as usual, which to me at that time was a blessing. Mother was at the kitchen table as usual with her cigarette and cup of tea. She had been waiting for my return as always; she was concerned about me and anxious to know what the doctor had said. When I saw Mother sitting at the table, I melted in her arms and cried like the baby I knew I had growing inside. I longed to be that little girl crying in her arms. I didn't want to be a big girl, I didn't want to be married, and I didn't want to be pregnant. Mother instinctively knew it was more than a bit of depression. I had to be honest and I had to tell Mother the story. As most children do, I was no different and blamed her for the mess I was in. I suggested if she had been more liberal and let me go, I wouldn't have gotten involved with the American or gone sneaking around. I reminded her that she never let me do anything. I was so hysterical, I could not communicate.

When I was able to pull it together long enough to be understood, I shared the news. There was a long pause and the air was heavy. What would she say? Would I be on the street, rejected and alone, or would she stand by me and support me? That had nothing to do with the other big hurdle I had to share with John. He would probably think he had married a slut just like the one he divorced. John would probably think I started sleeping around as soon as he left. He wouldn't believe me if I told him it was only one time. Would he reject me as well? I wanted to die.

When Mother finally spoke, she told me she would be there for me and hoped John would come to a place of understanding. The true love and bond of a mother is a powerful thing. I was confused and lost. I didn't know what the future would hold or how my life would unfold or what the journey would be. I did know my mother loved and supported me and that I had a new life growing in me.

I had nothing left from the events of the day and went to bed. I was exhausted but sleep did not come. I tossed and turned and listened to the winds from the sea. They seemed to be louder than usual. I finally got up and put pen to paper and began writing to John with the news. I wrote and rewrote letters, trying to find the words to explain or justify what I had done, praying he would still love me, want me, and give me a second chance. I remember the past he shared and the fact that he had fallen from grace. My sin was far more serious, as I had broken God's law. Could the love we had be strong enough to weather this storm? It was a big decision, but my love was true and I prayed John would understand how lonely I was. Regardless, I knew John would never find himself in my position. How was I to know John was being faithful and true to our vows? There was so much emotion and anxiety. I was thinking all kinds of scenarios.

I put it as best as I could on my tear-stained paper, expressing my love for him and longing for his touch. I told him the encounter was wrong and how very remorseful I was. I told him how I imagined it was him and not this nameless, faceless person. I told him it was only once that I fell from grace, and I prayed for his forgiveness. I gave him permission to reject me and this bastard child. I professed my love for him and desire to be with him. I told him I would be at his side as soon as the papers were approved if he would find forgiveness in his heart. I felt a strange sigh of relief as I lay in the darkness to drift off to slumber.

The next day, I wept as I dropped my letter at the post office, hoping for acceptance. I waited day after day for a reply as my body began changing, preparing for the birth of the child. Mother kept the news from Father and family, thinking they would presume I was with child from John. Mother was never judgmental and accepted life as it unfolded. I don't know if the family ever figured it out. It didn't matter; it was family and family gives unconditional love. They didn't speak of such matters. I wondered what this child was and what it would look like.

When I began to feel life, I felt peace and prayed for a healthy baby girl. I would name her Hope. I had no recollection of what the biological father looked like. It was all a blur.

The war had ended by now, and the British men were returning home. The Americans had left, but there were many women and babies left behind. There was a backlog of woman waiting for papers to go to the States.

I finally got a letter from my John. Mother actually got it in the post and handed it to me. I carried it around for three days before I had the courage to open it and read the contents. I was prepared for the two scenarios: acceptance and anticipation of my life in this new world, or rejection and remaining under the strong rule of my mother. Father accepted his fate and was resolved at his age to accept his life. He was finished. He never did return to work. I could never figure out how they managed with no income. Mother was very thrifty. There were no extras, and the good old days were a dim memory tucked safely away in my memory bank.

I went to our special rock at the sea by myself and opened the letter. I felt strong and protected in that place, my happy place. I knew whatever happened I would survive. Much to my surprise, the letter was sweet and supportive. While John was disappointed, he said he could understand how lonely and lost I must have felt when he left and actually apologized for having to leave me behind. John said he would accept this child and raise it as his own as long as the unknown biological father would never be a part of the child's life and professed his love and concern for me. He referred to me as his English rose. That request was not a problem since the biological father didn't know a baby even existed.

I felt like a warm blanket had been wrapped around me. I put my feet in the sea, knowing it was the same body of water that would touch his land. I felt a connection and purpose. I felt peace. I knew I could carry on and when my papers processed, I would be able to join John and bring this child and be a real family. With my spirits soaring, I walked home on air. It had been a very long time since I felt so enlightened. I knew I didn't have much time left before the birth, and the fear started to creep back in. I had no idea what to expect but knew it wouldn't be easy. Funny, when you are pregnant you move along and suddenly reality hits and you wonder how the little thing will get out. I had little money and would be having a home birth. No one can tell you what it's like or what to expect. Most births in England were home births. I thought, well, it was only a short time and I was creating life. You can do anything for a short time.

Mother had mixed emotions, knowing John would accept me with my bastard child and she would lose both of us to the other side of the world. There was little communication with John other than letters. Travel was days at sea by ship or hours by prop plane.

I woke one morning with a wet puddle in my bed. I called out to my mother, and she suggested I was beginning the birth process. She ran to summon the midwife as I lay waiting and anticipating what was happening. I knew it was a journey I was about to take alone. It was all about me and creating a miracle, the miracle of a new life. What would it be, a boy or a girl? I decided it would be a girl even though I had no reason to think so. I thought a girl would be easier for me if I were ever left alone. We could be special friends. I could dress her up like a babydoll and call her Faith. Faith: have it, hold on to it, believe in it. What would she look like? What did the father look like? There were so many mysteries.

I waited for what seemed like an eternity. I started to feel discomfort and just wanted it to be over. I waited and waited and waited. The pain grew worse and worse. I started bleeding profusely. I was convinced I deserved it for my mistake. I thought I would die for my sin right then and there.

The midwife finally arrived and checked me out. She determined I was to have a dry birth, which is difficult. I no longer cared about the miracle or responsibility and maybe deserved to die. Hours passed and I began to wish for death. Poor baby was a victim of this evil. I wanted to die, I deserved to die. I lay in that state for two days. I began to hallucinate, and Mother insisted I be transferred to the hospital. She feared for my life, as it seemed I was slipping away.

By the time I arrived at the hospital, I was at death's door. I figured it was the wrath of God and I deserved this fate, but so strong was my faith that I knew in my heart I was never alone. I was taken quickly to the operating room, and they took charge. I heard them say the birth would never have happened without medical intervention and this child, along with me, would not have made it. The incision was crude, as it had to be done quickly to save us. I was in more pain than I had ever had.

So there it was, finished. I was presented with a beautiful baby girl, Faith. She was perfect, although she had a struggle coming into the world. Faith had dark hair and big brown eyes just like John. I slipped into a dream world and imagined it was the child of John, a perfect love child. Such a blessing. It was love at first sight. Faith was beautiful. Oh, how I wished John had been at my side.

My head was spinning again. I was never good at math, and I figured when I got to the new land and reunited with John no one would figure it out. I sent a telegram to John with the baby news. Mother and Father were thrilled to welcome their first grandchild.

After a few days, we went back to the little flat but added another little person to the mix. I sent notification to John, and he was happy and anxious to meet the new little bundle of joy. I had to wait for the papers, which were still in process. I was inseparable with Faith. We slept together and I never left her. I was proud to walk her to the shops and grateful to have a tall, dark, handsome American father for her. I realized at that moment how and why my mother was so possessive. I wanted to keep Faith forever.

Mother and Father were the doting grandparents. It seemed like the perfect life but not really a good life for me and Faith. I wanted to run far away. The walls seemed like they were closing in faster and faster. I could see my future was not to be in that little flat. I wanted to go to America. I wanted to go to the New World. I wanted to be with my husband. I wanted his smell, his touch, his strength and support. I just wanted to go.

It was time. Letters continued to be exchanged, and John said he was anxious to see his English rose. I could feel the love, and it was real. That situation lasted eighteen months before my papers finally arrived. How difficult to leave your mother, take the first grandchild away, and disappear to the other side of the world. It is such a mistake to leave your country. There is so much more than just leaving. It's a culture shock. Mother was brokenhearted and sick, but Father communicated with me more in that brief period than he had in my whole life.

When the day to leave came, Father put a bit of money in my hand and told me I could come back at any time, and we would make it work. It was the first and only time I saw my father cry. Mother didn't speak much; she was too distraught to even speak. I boarded a bus to take to the ship that would take me to the new world. It was beginning of a great adventure. I looked out the window as the bus pulled away to see Mother running behind the bus weeping and Father, as stoic as he was, standing in the middle of the road like a broken old man. I suppose I should have felt some sadness, but I was so excited about my journey and after all, I had my baby, Faith, so I wasn't alone. I also had my tall, dark, handsome American husband waiting for me on the other side. I was too consumed with Faith and the adventure to realize how my family was left behind brokenhearted. Leaving had affected so many people, like a ripple in a pond. Mother ultimately suffered a severe case of shingles shortly after I left from the stress. What had I done? Had I committed yet another sin by leaving?

When we arrived at the ship, I had all my papers in order. There was mass confusion at the docks with all the other war brides and babies. Now I really didn't feel alone. We were all on the same ship with similar stories. Still, water runs deep.

The ship finally loaded and pulled away. I felt a little sadness and loss as I watched the shores of my beloved country disappear. It was a long journey, and the seas were rough. There were more sick babies and war brides than not. Many were ill and the babies got diarrhea.

Days went by before we pulled into the harbor in New York City. When we caught sight of Lady Liberty through the early-morning mist in the harbor, I knew we had arrived. I looked down at the face of my beautiful baby. *Faith,* I thought. *Such a perfect name for my child and my journey.* Faith: have it, hold it, believe it.

I was about to jump out of my skin with anticipation. It took hours to process everyone on the ship through Ellis Island. The officials boarded and inquired if anyone had a child with diarrhea. I had a white knit suit on Faith. I knew if I told them she did in fact have an issue, we would be quarantined for who knew how long. I lied again; it seemed to be a pattern of lies. Faith did have a problem but I feared isolation, so I told them she was okay and they trusted my answer. I knew John was waiting and would be concerned if we didn't get off the ship. I was motioned off the ship and free to go.

There was a sea of people—nameless, faceless people. Unlike the rough sea we had just crossed, little did I know what lay before me and how my journey would go. My sea of life was about to get rougher than the sea I just crossed. It was exciting to see all the happy reunions, and my eyes scanned the sea of faces, looking and looking. Where was John and why wasn't he there? I was scared. I didn't see a familiar face. There I was. I had arrived to no one, nowhere. I sad on a bench with my Faith and cried. I didn't know what else to do. They were tears from heaven. I called out to my dear grandmother in my head. I could feel her presence and thought I would make it. She would be there to guide and protect me through divine intervention. I knew I had to be strong for Faith and myself and looked for inner strength to see me through. Had John reflected and changed his mind? What was I to do? How could I turn back now? It was the beginning of a great adventure.

An official approached me and offered to assist me. I told him my story, which was not like the rest coming off the ship. Mine was different because there was no one to meet me. I was lost. He looked at my papers and asked where I was going. I said I wasn't sure but the ending location was somewhere in the Midwest. He told me to be strong and directed me to the train station. He instructed me to board the train to Chicago.

When I arrived there, I was to travel on another train to a little Midwest town in the middle of the country. At that point I wanted to get back on that ship and go home. I didn't want to do this. I wanted to go back to my comfort zone, back to my country, back to my family, back to what I knew, familiarity. I knew I was at the point of no return. I was committed to continue my journey. So onward I went with my precious Faith, my reason for living and my future. Faith was my rock and the only thing that kept me grounded.

I got to Chicago to a scene much like the one that greeted me in New York. Still, no familiar face. I was lost, confused, tired, and hungry. Where in the world was I? I thought, *Dear God, why have you forsaken me?* At least as a nursing mother, I knew Faith was okay. I just wanted a cup of tea. Tea always makes you feel better.

I boarded yet another train to a little Midwest city in the middle of the country. The land of opportunity, they called it. Well, not mine. After numerous stops in little cities, my city name was announced and I got off the train. I had never felt so lost and alone, but Faith needed me and I had to be strong. I scanned the platform looking for my handsome soldier. There was a small group of homeless-looking people on the platform. They were natives of the area. I heard my name called from a familiar voice. When I responded, I realized within the small group was John dressed in overalls and my "new family" in the new land. There was my mother-in-law, an old lady in a cotton dress with an apron, and others who looked as if they had just come from working the land. My feet seemed to be stuck to the ground, and I didn't want to move toward this group and life. Wow, I was taken aback.

Although it was not the sharp, tall, dark, handsome soldier in his uniform, it was my husband. When we embraced, all the feelings were there. John still had those beautiful dark eyes that looked deep into my soul, those same eyes I had fallen in love with. Looking deep into his eyes as we engaged without words, it simply reassured me I would be okay and John would be the rock foundation to build on. The peace that passes all understanding washed over me, and it was good.

I stuck close to my John. Where was I going, where were we going to live? When could I be alone with my John? So many questions, so few answers. Little did I know my journey had just begun. They were good God-fearing people. It was a large family, as my John was a child of eight. I never met his father, as he had passed away from some disease years before. He was, however, a salesman and seldom around unless it was short visits, which usually resulted in another mouth to feed.

My new mother-in-law was a loving yet tough woman. She was of German descent, tough and determined. Meeting her explained where John had gotten his tough and determined spirit. Her life was working the farm alone and caring for her family. They were typical farm people. I think perhaps they had many children to work the fields. She gave birth in that farmhouse alone and got the family bible out to name the new life. One story was told how she gave birth to twins, then went into the field just after to work.

Another where she broke her leg, made it back to the house, set it with two sticks, and then made dinner for the family. Nothing went to waste—even the cloth bags the flour came in were opportunities for new dresses for the girls in the family. It was the only life she knew and the way she thought life was. They were happy.

Life was simple with simple pleasures. Fresh fruit and a few nuts in a stocking were typical Christmas gifts. Church was what you did on Sunday. There was routine, structure, and great respect. Every child learned an instrument, and country music was the entertainment—not the stuff you hear today, but whiny country music that usually told a story of doom and gloom. John played mandolin, piano, harmonica, and accordion—even Mama played the spoons and the younger ones would bang on pans or washboards with spoons. Everyone played by ear. There was no instruction or lessons. There was dancing and singing. I was so complicated and unhappy. It was strange and could not have been more different from the life I knew and left behind.

School was unstructured; it was a one-room building miles from the farm. It was a privilege to be able to go to school, and the long walk back and forth was never considered a problem. No one complained, even with the bite of winter. Besides, it was an opportunity to be with friends and a break from the many chores. I met my new family, and they embraced Faith and me with love and support. They couldn't quite figure out my accent; however, they were so intrigued by it, they simply wanted me to keep talking. I supposed they thought I was speaking a foreign language. I thought they were speaking a foreign language as well. Many British phrases didn't translate well. "Chips" to me were French fries, "crisps" were potato chips, a biscuit was a cookie, a tart was a hooker, knickers were underpants, and a fag was a cigarette. I was promptly correctly when I told them one day to keep their pecker up. To me it meant "keep your spirits up." One can only imagine my embarrassment when it was translated and it revealed as dirty talk. There was plenty of that, and I didn't understand it.

I didn't want to talk. I wanted to be alone with John and Faith. I wanted to go home. I wanted to see where my life would be. I wanted a cup of tea. I wanted a bath and to get into bed with John's loving arms around me.

After some introductions, we traveled to the home of my new mother-in-law. We turned onto a dirt road, which led to a long driveway back to a small farmhouse. This was where we were to begin our life? Everything was strange. It was a culture shock at all angles from the time I had left England to the day I met Lady Liberty. My life was about to change dramatically, if not already, and nothing in my entire life could even be imagined. I tried to be positive but knew I was in deep trouble after a brief tour of the house. When I asked for the toilet, I was directed to an even smaller house a few yards from the main house. It was the toilet, aka outhouse. A small wooden lean to when you opened the door, there was a bench with two round holes cut. Was this their idea of two bathrooms? It was obvious how it got the name since you didn't have to look for it but smell your way to it. I made my John come with me and stand watch when I had the need to go to the little house. You certainly never took a paper to read; you took care of business and quickly. The cold mornings or night nature calls were especially quick. I imagined some animal might jump out of the hole and I would die right there on the spot. I just wanted to cry and get back on that train, remembering my father's words, that I could always return. Tea, tea, where was the tea? I was frightened for Faith and myself.

The die was cast, and I wondered if this was my punishment for my adulteress sin. I thought I had a taste of hell, and yet our love was true and strong and, I thought, enough to sustain me and get me over the top of my mountain. I kept repeating in my head, *Faith: have it, hold it, believe in it.* I would gaze at the bright stars in the dark Midwest country sky and talk to my dear grandmother in my head, sure that she was there looking down on me. I knew she had a special star. I thought I was losing my mind. Maybe I was. Faith always pulled me back to reality. There were copious amounts of fresh food, but it looked strange. The green beans were no longer green but a brown color from being overcooked. Everything was mushy. All I craved was a good cup of tea. Tea always made you feel better. There was no tea, and any effort to make a cup of tea was not like home. Tea has to be made from very hot water and steeped before adding milk. These people had a lot to learn about my country, and yet all they wanted to do was to hear me talk. I suppose I had a lot to learn about this country as well.

It was winter. Winter in the Midwest is very cold and bitter. England had lots of rain but not the cold temperatures. English babies are exposed to fresh air every day. Maybe that's why they always look so rosy. It's not from being particularly healthy but rather chapped. I didn't realize you couldn't put a baby outside in the fresh air when that air was freezing. I pushed Faith in her pram outside every day for a nap just as I had done in England. John was cautioned by the family to address that habit, as they feared for the safety of the baby. I struggled to adapt and go with the flow, but every day brought more and more challenges and I started to slip into a deeper depression.

My new family was giving me instructions on canning. Seems this is what you do and it keeps you in food for the winter. It was like a foreign language. Actually, I guess it was a foreign language. I remember one particular Christmas, my mother-in-law always cooked for the family but by this time her children had scattered around the country. One daughter disappeared with her possessive husband and was never found. They thought he killed her and threw her off a mountain in the West somewhere. Anyway, there were gifts for everyone under the tree. When I opened my gift, I saw that someone had made me a set of hot pads. Oh, they were very special. There was a male and a female hot pad. Both had aprons on and when you lifted the apron on the male, there was a penis, and the female had lots of black yarn that looked like pubic hair. I quickly put them back in the box for disposal the minute I got home. The family thought it was very funny. That was just one example of the many family situations I found myself in. I was a proper, reserved English girl and couldn't relate to these farm people. They attempted to teach me, but it was a struggle at every turn. I was not only learning to cook their way but learning to navigate through a kitchen as well. That was my mother's area, and she never shared her skills with me. My mother's kitchen was sacred ground, and I spent little time there. She just took care of us. I wanted her to take care of me now. I wanted my mother.

Everything was fried in pig lard—even the vegetables. If they weren't fried, they were cooked long enough to lose their color. You couldn't even recognize what vegetables they were at times. I did learn how to fry food, but it was never the golden brown color they achieved. I learned to fry chicken after I cut the head off and cleaned it first. The chickens would run around after their head was cut off, splattering blood everywhere. You had to take caution on wash day, when clothes were hung out to dry. Wash day was never the same as the day you cut off chickens heads. I always liked chickens; they seemed to happy just pecking around on the ground. I was careful not to bond with the chickens or give them names. I couldn't imagine eating a pet. They had to remain nameless and faceless just like the father of Faith.

I thought spending the day in the car while John worked was preferred to being left behind. Diapers were also a challenge. I would wash the soiled ones as best I could and hang them out to dry. In the winter months they would freeze, and I had to put them near an open fire to warm up and get soft. Just as I thought I was about to lose my mind, I had a heart-to-heart conversation with John. Poor John was such a good man and a hard worker. John tried so hard to make me happy. I never realized until the end of my life journey how blessed I was. Like looking through a dirty window, you don't realize how dirty it is until you clean it.

John was seldom around, working two jobs and leaving me with the family. My heart skipped a beat when John would come home from work, but the visit was brief, as John would dash out to take advantage of any sunlight left to work on our little house. When John finally did come home, he was too tired to have any intimacy I so craved. I often fell asleep in tears. I was never comfortable with that aspect in his mother's home anyway. There was little to no privacy, and Faith slept in a crib next to our bed. John promised he would build a house on the land next to the family farm for the three of us. He promised one day he would be a millionaire. John promised lots of things, which was the only thing that kept my sanity—that and Faith, for whom I knew I had to be strong. John was a self-made man with not much formal education. The German roots he had gave him the drive and determination to get what he wanted and where he wanted to go. Education came from outside life lessons rather than the classroom with a useless piece of paper. John was brilliant and driven. I wanted to run away, but I loved my husband and I knew I had made that decision long ago and there was nothing to go back to.

By now my sister, Scarlett, had married and had a child, so it was a full house and certainly no room for me. What could I do to support Faith and myself if I were to return to England? One thing sure was the love John had for me and acceptance of a child he didn't father. It was a constant reminder of my infidelity. John had a child as well, but it was well within the boundaries of marriage and commitment. I tried to make excuses but knew I was a sinner. So I decided I needed to hang tough and deal with my situation as best I could.

The house was built and we moved into it. It was very small but cozy, and it was the three of us. We were independent. There was even an inside toilet. Ahh, what a luxury. We had our own space, and the intimacy that was so important in our marriage returned. The things you take for granted until they are taken away.

I was in heaven but only briefly. It wasn't enough. It was never enough. John kept working two jobs and was seldom home. Now I didn't even have extended family to interact with—I was really alone. There were days I never opened my mouth. It was such a solitary life—an ideal environment for depression to grow. It was dark at night and when it stormed, I was petrified. I had never seen storms like that. I took Faith and sat in a corner until the storm passed. I thought perhaps I would be blown away and maybe land back in England. I kept slipping lower and lower. I craved an English biscuit or anything British, a friend, good music. Oh, I got the tea issue solved since I now had my own little space. I took any opportunity to get out. I never learned to drive. Few people did in England. The trams, trains, and buses got you where you needed to go. Marketing was done on a daily basis. Every shop had its specialty, from the meat market to the cake shops, sweet shops, and everything in between.

Eventually I was introduced to another war bride. She had quite a different story to tell. Many of the war brides had a much tougher time than me. They had little choice but to accept their life as it was. This particular bride married a very jealous man. She lived in a modified garage. When she thought he had gone to work, he would circle back and peer through the window to be sure she wasn't with another man. She was living in a box world. I felt blessed even though I was so very homesick and lonely. I thought I would lose my mind again before I had another talk with John and asked that we move to the "city." I needed people and activity. As usual, in an attempt to make me happy, John went on a hunt to find a house in the city. John tried everything and did everything to fill the void. Now this city, as I call it, was a small Midwest city, but there were people, families and activities, and shops. They even had an organization called the Cosmopolitan Club, which was compromised of war brides just like me—girls from my country who understood me, people who sounded like me.

We packed up and moved to the city. It was a good move, and John was glad after all to move to the city. It was the first time since John has been in England that he had left the farm. John continued working long hours, eager to make that million he promised. John thought the only path that made sense was to have his own business. He loved messing around with chemicals and developed some formulas for cleaning products. John worked hard building the business one dollar at a time. Once a week, he drove his truck to a neighboring town to sell his products. I'm not sure if he was faithful. I questioned myself and thought perhaps I wasn't enough to keep him satisfied. I was so unhappy, and the only thing that seemed to give me any happiness and peace was the physical intimacy with John. It was the same magic that made the bond and gave me the strength to make the decisions I made. Love is blind, but it's also stupid and sometimes lacks common sense.

I was introduced to an older couple. They were childless and took me under their wing. They loved the way I talked and tried to fill the void. They were good Christian people. I really needed a friend. They invited me to go to their church. I jumped at the invitation, thinking I would go anywhere. The last church and service I had attended was the Church of England in my country. That was all I knew and thought church to be. The Church of England is a high church, very conservative and proper. This experience was strange. The church was a Nazarene church, and I couldn't imagine anything like this existed. The enthusiasm of the congregation was great, but when they started to shout out and roll on the floor, I thought they were all experiencing demons or some sort of medical issue, then realized an entire church wouldn't be ill. I decided to accept it for what it was and considered it an outing. I figured the Holy Spirit was on them. It was yet another language to understand when some began speaking in tongue; however, everyone was inviting and kind. I hoped one day to join a conservative church on a regular basis with Faith and John. It was important to me to have that connection. Religious faith and structure not only binds a family but also lays a foundation for children to build on for a lifetime of their own journey.

After a short time in our new home in the city, I got sick. I tried to cope but got sicker and sicker. Something seemed somewhat familiar. I asked to be taken to a doctor and was diagnosed with an unexpected pregnancy. I was beside myself with fear. A flood of memories from the prior birthing experience with Faith came back. The circumstances were very different from the birth of Faith in England. John would be by my side this time, and I knew in my heart he would never leave me. I flipped out and thought for sure I would die. When I accepted the concept of a new life, any joy I had feeling life in me was overcome with fear. I spent my entire pregnancy filled with anxiety. Pregnant, okay, wonderful, but how would this new life get out of me? I had nine months to think about it. What was to become of Faith? Who would love and care for her like me in my brief absence when the time came to give birth? I prayed God would not forsake me in my hour of need. It seemed I was calling for divine intervention all too frequently.

I asked for the best doctor in the town, anticipating the same dreadful experience. The staff and physician could not have been nicer. I went through that pregnancy with two dresses: one for home and one for when I went for my doctor's appointments. I was too preoccupied mentally and physically to worry about anything else. I was so careful and had an uneventful pregnancy. This was a love child, conceived in love. I had this bastard child, and he had an unknown son, but this was special. How could anything go wrong? I had good food and a supportive family around me.

As my delivery date approached, I began to worry about Faith. We had never been separated. New mommies and babies stayed in the hospital seven to ten days. That was an eternity. By now Faith was bonded with John. I knew John loved Faith and Faith loved John. I was assured she would be well cared for, and yet again that choice was made for me. I had to pray she would be safe.

One morning I awoke to a wet bed. I dreamed I was out to sea on my way back to England. When I came back to reality, I realized my water had broken and I was going into labor. The plan was put into place. Faith was taken to my mother-in-law in the country on our way to the hospital. John was not allowed anywhere near the delivery room, and again it was a solo journey. This experience had nothing similar with my previous one. It went on without incident.

I delivered a beautiful baby girl quickly. How fun, I thought, to have two girls. How I treasured the relationship I had with my sister, Scarlett, growing up, and what a gift this child was, not only from above but also to our earthly family. What a wonderful gift of a sibling. I don't think I would have made the choice to have another child, but again, the choice was not mine. I think it's a gift to have two children. They learn so much from one another about sharing and giving. I was thrilled with my beautiful baby and named her Joy. She would be the joy in my life that had been missing.

I had enough milk for a roomful of babies and had no issues nursing. The nurse was not happy with me when I noticed one of her ears was down on the top. She reminded me how perfect Joy was and I had no reason to complain. I enjoyed all the attention and fuss at the hospital but longed to see Faith. I hoped she was okay.

John brought her to the hospital and let her wave to me from the sidewalk. It must have seemed like an eternity to Faith. Faith probably felt abandoned. Oh, how I wanted to jump out of the window and embrace her. Faith stood on the sidewalk, waving her little hands, crying out to me, not understanding why I couldn't get to her or her to me. I cried for Faith and was anxious to leave the hospital with Joy. John mentioned Faith was a little constipated, so they were thinking of giving her an enema. I went into such a rage that they promised they would not. Evidently it was routine for country people to do that with children. It was routine in England to add a few stewed prunes to the diet for constipation. I prayed they would not violate Faith or touch her little bottom. I couldn't wait for the day to be released and reunited.

Finally Joy and I were released from the hospital and went home. Another child added to the mix didn't improve my increasing depression. I was so homesick. There were phones and I phoned my family on an occasional basis, but it was difficult at best. It was expensive, so the calls were brief and the connection was poor. My mother just cried and cried and wanted me to talk so she could hear my voice. My goodness, everyone it seemed just wanted to hear me talk.

My good Nazarene friends, Adele and Floyd, were a big part of our lives. When I would purge closets, I would pass on out-of-style ties to Floyd. When skinny ties were in fashion, I would give the fat ones and vice versa. Floyd was always in style, just not always at the appropriate time. They were a funny little couple, so overweight. They just waddled along like two little potato heads. They often came by about dinnertime and when an invitation to stay was extended, they would refuse the invitation but accept it gladly in the end.

John worked and worked and the girls were not enough to keep me focused, so I asked to seek counseling to cope with my many life changes and depression. Perhaps I suffered some postpartum depression, along with depression from the culture shock. It was never really diagnosed. One day Faith turned the bassinet and Joy over. I heard a thud and just saw a heap of blankets with Joy on the floor. Perhaps that was a sign of things to come? I did make a series of appointments with a counselor and got dropped off for an hour on a regular basis to share my woes and come to a place of understanding. It was exhausting, as I would pour my heart out. The counselor simply listened and waited for his fee. He seemed insensitive and didn't appear to understand. It was a waste of time and money we didn't have, but it was an outlet. I thought a complete stranger would get a clearer picture of my feelings and be able to offer some advice and suggestions.

John didn't know what else he could do to make me happy. The bottom line was always the same; the counselor suggested there was nothing wrong other than an extreme case of homesickness. It was advised I should get a job, fill my life with more friends, and not be in so much isolation. But this time the girls were about to start school. I needed to go home (England). I needed to see my family. I needed to step out of this life to appreciate it. There was little exchange, just me talking and the counselor listening. The counselor was non-judgmental. I could probably have talked to the wall or a frog in the back garden, accomplish the same, and save the fee. I knew I had to be strong for the girls. It was an important part of my recovery. It wasn't just about me.

We were not in a position to afford the trip to England but made it happen. I left a brokenhearted man as I departed with the girls, telling John I didn't know if I would come back. At that point, I didn't know if I was coming back. It was the first time I had seen my brave, strong man cry. How could I hurt someone I loved and he love me unconditionally? Guess I had it in me since I had done the same with my family when I left England. I was sad and ashamed of my actions but knew this was the only way to settle my head and heart and make me a better wife and mother for John. I knew this would be the turning point. I looked forward with anticipation. I was torn between two worlds. I would always be stuck between two worlds, not having a sense of belonging to either. I was anxious to see my family and even my cranky old father, Dick. I wanted to eat and drink all the food I had craved for so long. I wanted to be mothered. I wanted to reunite Faith with the family and introduce my Joy.

Faith, Joy, and I boarded a propjet for the long flight across the pond. I looked out the tiny airplane window to see John weeping as we taxied down the runway and disappeared. It made me sad. As the plan began its descent and I saw the ground and English countryside, I started to cry uncontrollably. It was home, I was home! Oh, how I had missed my country.

We took a bus from the airport to my home village and my family. They accepted us with open arms. They looked different, not the family I grew up with or left. Mother and Dad were aging rapidly. Father was a different man from what I remembered or grew up with. He was mellow and such a proud grandfather. From the moment I stepped into the bungalow, I had the answer to my questions. I knew I had no choice but to return to the new land and my life. It was very clear my life was with John. My sister, Scarlett, had since married and had a child and it was very crowded in that little bungalow. Mother had aged as she recovered from shingles brought on when I left. Father had mellowed out, and age was taking him as well. He was a nicer, kinder, gentler man than the one I had grown up with. It was nice to see that side of him and know it existed. I secretly wished I had that father and side when I grew up and needed him. That was a lifetime ago, and I had to let it go. There's a window raising children, which makes it such an awesome responsibility. It's not a do-over, so you try not to make too many mistakes. It is such a dynamic impact on the life you hold in the palm of your hand when you have children.

Mother was thrilled to have me and her two beautiful grandchildren back under the same roof. I know now how much I must have hurt her and how difficult I had made her life. It was a reality check how much my mother meant to me and how I could not imagine life without her or what I would have felt if my children left me as I did her. I was ashamed of what I had done. I enjoyed our visit and all the English foods and tradition. I enjoyed being mothered and observing the joy my girls brought as they engaged with "my" family. I realized how starved I was for good music. There were no classics on the radio and only hardcore country music, not the country music of today but the whiny kind with sad stories told in the lyrics. I realized if change were to happen, I had to be the change.

The bungalow looked even smaller than I had remembered, and I remembered the home I had left in American with John. I was looking with different eyes and could see clearly. My life was beginning to focus. I left that visit with a changed attitude and positive attitude. I had nothing to be depressed or sad about. I was blessed.

We returned to the arms of a loving, strong husband and father. John was so happy, you would think he had won the lottery. It made me feel loved and wanted, and I vowed to change a few things, including my attitude.

The girls started school, and I got a little part-time job to get out of the house and be near people. I didn't like feeling isolated. My entire life was about the girls and John. I didn't want the walls to start closing again. I worked when the girls were in school. Finding work was easy. My English accent always opened doors, and potential employers just wanted to hear me talk. I quickly took a part-time secretarial job. I was there when the girls left for school and when they came home. It was wonderful to get up and have a purpose and place to go. I liked getting dressed up and going to a working environment, engaging with intelligent people. They were educated, high-class people, the sort mother came from. I liked being in the working world, and getting a little check was always a bonus. It gave me a sense of pride. It was a good, simple life—very safe.

We got a second car, and I learned to drive. I had a couple of small mishaps along the way, including hitting the garbage can, garage, and the milk box, but nothing serious, and John took it in stride, always supportive and understanding. My mental counseling sessions were replaced by citizenship with England, so I was still connected to the motherland. I didn't have to make a choice. The citizenship course was difficult, and I had to learn and remember a lot before I took the exam. I had no support along the way, and no American I spoke with knew much about their government. If they had been given the exam I took, they would have surely failed. I did take the exam at the end of the course and passed on my first attempt. I was granted citizenship and given a small American flag. Funny, I still didn't feel I belonged, but I didn't know where I belonged. I was stuck between two worlds and would always be.

I joined a group of British war brides. It was interesting to exchange stories and have a built-in support group that I felt really understood me. They were girls who could relate to me and my feelings. Support groups are always successful, like a bird that needs two wings to fly. It also reminded me how blessed I was when I looked at my life. Many of the women had to endure physical and mental abuse and their men knew they could do nothing about it. The woman did not have education and could not find work that would pay them enough to support themselves and their children. They were really stuck. It was a reality check, and I was grateful and felt settled.

I started to turn around and feel better about myself and my life. I was even able to find a radio station that played classical music. We joined the Methodist church and got involved with the Masonic temple. John was a mason and proud of it. That was another social outlet for us. The girls would play with the neighbors and go out after dinner until dark. We didn't lock cars and houses and never feared strangers. There was no internet or sexual predators. There were family potlucks, but my fried chicken was never as brown and crispy as the others. They always knew which chicken was mine. The girls moved through school at their own pace. They didn't have or get much support since I never really understood the educational system. Luckily they were bright enough to figure it out.

We began vacationing in Florida on a yearly basis. I longed for the sea. Perhaps it was one of the comments my mother had made. I remember Mother telling me when I left she would go to the sea and put her feet in the water, knowing in a funny way it was the same body of water that would touch me and connect us. I used to think the same when I was waiting for my papers to join John after he left me in England. Oh, what a heartache I caused.

By this time, John's business had formed a partnership with two other men. On one particular trip to Florida, when we returned the door to the business was locked and the locks changed. The other two men had voted John out, and he was now on the outside looking in to a business he had started. John was devastated. It was a do-over at his age, but John was touch and determined. John walked the streets, going from bank to bank looking for a loan to start up again. With every step came disappointment and rejection. No one would take a chance or grant him a start-up loan. John was very guarded with his secret formulas and carried that information with him. With no luck, money, or hope, John turned to a loan shark. I didn't get into his business, so I didn't know the nice men who were invited into our home were actually taking inventory of every stick of furniture. I was told little other than it was business and John was taking care of it. I didn't question it and trusted John.

John was able to tread water long enough to surface again. He learned a valuable lesson and never had another partner. His new business actually closed the business that screwed him. They didn't have the products or formulas to compare with his and were unable to compete. John was desperate for that million-dollar promise. He finally paid off the loan shark. It was a climb out of a big hole.

As time passed, my adulteress past never did. I buried that secret but could never come to a place where I could move past it. It ate me like a cancer. Perhaps I should have been honest about it from the beginning, but it was far beyond that as this point. Faith was now about to finish high school. She started to look different than anyone on either side of the family. Her teeth were crooked and she had a funny shape. The differences were becoming more obvious as the years went by that she didn't belong genetically to this family. There was nothing even similar to John. I felt an obligation to tell Faith the truth. I had "the talk" with John again and announced I needed to see my family. I told John he must tell Faith the truth about her nameless, faceless father and I was taking "our child," Joy, to England and not coming back until I knew he had delivered the news.

Unfortunately this was not John's news. It was my mistake and responsibility, but I simply did not have the strength or courage to tell Faith. John had to reveal my secret that he was not her biological father and she was the product of a one-night stand with a nameless, faceless person. John was to reassure Faith that he had accepted her as his own and raised her as his and loved her unconditionally. This truth would answer the mystery to Faith why she looked different. I don't really know how or what was said or the reaction Faith had. Guess it wasn't my business, and I had no right to know since I put that on John. I know I spent my life attempting to make up to Faith for my fall from grace. I was sorry and ashamed that I was unable to provide Faith with any information about her roots. I didn't know them. Faith was about to finish high school and didn't want to go to England, so the timing seemed right.

Things were the same when I returned, but there was the addition of a small dog. I presume it was a peace offering when John delivered the news. Anyway, nothing was ever said and life went on. Faith never confronted me or asked any questions. Faith and I had a special bond. It probably didn't matter to her at that point. John was the only father she knew, and she loved him. There was never a time Faith was made to feel different even though she looked different.

Shortly after I returned from England with Joy, I got a letter informing me my father had suffered a stroke and died. Funny, although I cried when I read the news, I didn't feel anything. Perhaps it was just too late to establish a relationship that was never there. You should feel something when you lose a parent, but it just didn't happen. I didn't feel a need to return home and knew Mother would be okay. After all, my sister, Scarlett, never left home. I knew Scarlett would never leave Mother.

Faith was dating a boy for years, her high school sweetheart. He was a Catholic. Perhaps not Mr. Right, but Mr. Right Now. Joy met a young man just finishing his degree as she entered the university after high school graduation. It was a love match for Joy with her soulmate, Hunter. Hunter went into the military after graduation. Joy dropped out after one college semester and returned home. She was far too young to go away to college and didn't have the discipline or support to succeed. The courtship with Hunter was brief, and it was announced they were getting married. Joy was only eighteen, but I remember my growing-up years and all the limitations my mother put on me. I didn't want to inflict that on my Joy. Hunter was a nice young man, adored Joy, had a good education, and was being taken care of by the military, so we gave our blessing. Faith was not to be upstaged by her younger sister and pressured her boyfriend into marriage. Both girls were married and left within months of one another. I was alone again.

John had his own business working toward that million dollars one dollar at a time. I gave John an ultimatum. I told him I would not live my life in what I affectionately referred to as the armpit of the nation. I needed to be by the sea. When I think of it, I had put John's back to the wall too many times. I suppose it was a confirmation and testament to the love he had for me and I was just too clueless to see. I was on the move and John was welcome to come or not. After living so many years in America, I felt strong and independent and thought I could do or go anywhere. I knew I had the strength. I felt like a caterpillar morphed into a butterfly. I repeated that all too familiar phrase: faith, have it, hold it, believe in it. I thought of the many sacrifices and experiences I endured through my life for John, and now it was John's turn to make some adjustments.

John was very close to his mother, but she passed soon after the girls married. Not wanting to lose his English rose, John sold the business and our home and bought a semi truck with everything we owned and headed south. That little town was the only place John had ever known. It was a good move for everyone, and John never looked back. He thanked me numerous times throughout the next years for getting him out. It was yet another do-over, as John started another successful business in Florida. He returned to his hometown only once, when his sister was beat up at the hands of her son and lay at death's door.

Faith moved to Chicago. I wasn't a fan of her spouse. He was a banker, very tight with the money, and he wanted to isolate Faith from her family. Some years after the marriage, it was revealed a few days before the wedding he presented her with papers to be signed for any children brought to the marriage be raised Catholic. There was an ultimatum attached stating there would be no wedding if she didn't sign the paper. Faith was never a strong person and did not make good decisions. Maybe that was my fault, as I was always fixing her life. I thought it was my responsibility to her for my mistake. That marriage ultimately failed after the death of their baby girl. I think it was doomed from the start. You can't base a relationship and marriage on lies. Guess I dodged the bullet on that since I was living one very big lie. Faith was working in the city and slipped on the ice when she was pregnant. The umbilical cord detached and when the premature baby was delivered, she was too weak to survive and died. Faith never recovered from the loss of her child.

After the delivery, Faith was put in a room across from the nursery until they moved her to a different floor. The baby was named since it was a live birth, and the father took the tiny casket in the back of his car to our little town for a Catholic burial with his family. Perhaps it was payback for his insensitivity. After that marriage fell apart, Faith had an affair with the neighbor. When Faith made the decision to make the break and end the marriage, she left in a snowstorm driving 100 mpg on icy roads to Florida. She had no money or sense. Faith phoned and was told to get a room and stay where she was, and her "father," John, was on his way to see her through the rest of the journey. John dropped everything and took the next plane to fly to her side, and they drove the rest of the way together. It was not his biological child, but John assumed all responsibility for her and loved her.

When Faith got to Florida, she buried herself in the bedroom. Joy, on the other hand, spent four years in Washington, D.C., with Hunter. Hunter left the military and had since moved to Florida. The divorce for Faith was finalized, and she wanted nothing from the marriage. Faith even rejected the diamond, which I put away for safe keeping. The only time I can recall John rejecting Faith was one incident when the neighbor from Chicago came to Florida for a visit and Faith spent time with him at a local motel. John was disgusted and didn't speak to Faith. That affair was short lived when the neighbor returned to his wife and life. Why so much infidelity in my life? Is that genetic? Faith slipped into a depression and only came out when it was time to eat. She had no responsibilities in the house and was going nowhere. Faith was still young enough to start over, but it had to be her decision. I think perhaps that was the turning point for her faith or lack of. She always blamed God for anything that went wrong in her life. She threw pity parties and always played the victim.

Faith was encouraged to get a job. Reluctantly Faith interviewed at a local bank for a teller position. The human resource officer, Jim, was recently divorced. Jim was ten years older. Faith got more than just the job she applied for. Jim began pursuing her. Marriage came soon after. Jim was a mean, selfish, self-absorbed man and put her on a tight budget. Faith asked for the diamond ring from her first husband I had kept since Jim had given Faith a simple gold band. I'm sure Jim was proud for Faith to wear the big diamond, people believing he had given it to her. A year after the marriage came a baby boy. Jim had three children from a prior marriage that ended in divorce after he caught his then-wife with another man. Jim was estranged from his children. They played the game "If I can't have what I want, then I won't see you." That didn't work for the banker, so he cut the ties. Jim seemed okay with not having contact with his children, although they tried to reach out to him, only to be rejected. There was only one child born in that marriage for Faith, so the void was always there for a girl.

Jim was much like her previous mate and wanted to alienate her from the family. The bonds were too strong to be broken. Jim put Faith on an allowance and Faith spent it buying the best food for Jim, denying herself of anything she wanted. Joy told Faith to buy hot dogs for Jim rather than steak. There were numerous social functions with the bank that included golf and fancy dinners and drinking. Faith was uncomfortable in that world and aspect of life and preferred to stay in the shadows. Faith had little self-confidence, and I wasn't there to be her crutch.

Faith was very possessive of her boy, Don, and "fixed" his life at all costs. Don ultimately got involved in the drug world. That was a secret Faith kept from Jim. Faith kept a lot from Jim. She was a psycho mom. If Don didn't like a teacher, Faith found a different teacher. If Don didn't want to do something, he didn't have to do it. Don was unable to even speak for himself. If you tried to have a conversation with him, Faith would finish his sentences and answer for him. If Don didn't want to go to dinner with the family, then he would stay home alone with a bag of fast food.

The turning point for Don came at an early age. Done would rough house with his dad until Jim found himself on the floor one time and that activity abruptly ended. Jim dreamed of the day his son would play football. Don tried to play football to please his dad but found himself on the ground a few times and obviously had no interest or ability. Don expressed a desire to play basketball. He was quite tall and really wanted to play. Jim turned his back on him and told him basketball was for black boys. That began a downward spiral of rejection and limitations I knew all too well.

Don was busted for dealing and using drugs. He even had his hand stabbed, probably in a drug deal gone bad. Don was incarcerated a couple of times, but Faith fixed it as usual. I felt sorry for Faith and her situation. I secretly paid her credit card bills several times to help her out, still feeling some obligation and responsibility for her. I don't think I did her any favors. Faith never knew how to cope without my help and support and knew I would always be there to bail her out. It was basic. I never taught her how to fish but provided her with fish.

Although Joy was married at such a young age, her marriage was strong. Her husband, Hunter, provided well and their house was happy. My two girls had a good relationship most of their lives. Joy, after eight years, had a surprise pregnancy and surprise twin girls. That didn't sit well with Faith, as her heart still ached for that daughter that never was. When Joy went into premature labor to deliver, it was John at her side. John dropped everything to rush to the hospital for the birth. When it was announced Joy delivered not one but two girls, I knew I made the right decision to stay with Faith at the business in the office rather than meet my new grand-daughters. It was like salt in an open wound to Faith. While she was happy to welcome the girls and be an aunt, it was a bitter pill. That family was quite different. The twins were raised in a strong faith-based home, given a private Christian education, and went on to college and graduated. The class structure I grew up with was instilled in that home, and I was proud to see the values instilled in another generation. I knew my dear mother would have been proud.

We had family gatherings but only when it was necessary. Faith and Jim thought family consisted of three people. They had big dogs that ate from the family plates. Joy and the twins refused to go to her home. We spent a lot of time with Joy. When the girls came along, we were able to engage with them on a regular basis. They would pop over several times a week to share the girls with us. It was a special time I would cherish. We seldom sat for the girls and preferred to just be with them. John and I were blessed to spend those short, precious days with the girls. It was family, the way I grew up and the way I thought it was to be. Even my life in the "new land" was always family. Sundays were church, pot roast afterwards for lunch, and a visit with my mother-in-law.

One of my fondest memories was a last journey to England. Joy put a trip together. John, Joy, Hunter, and I stayed in various country manor houses. The manor homes used to be private estates, but the upkeep forced many of them to open as a bed and breakfast to generate enough income to enable them to keep their property. We took a short drive to the manor house of my uncle, where I had spent many happy days. It was a place I could close my eyes and imagine I was in when I needed to escape reality. I wish I had never made that journey and kept it the beautiful memory I had.

The drive to the top of the hill revealed an overgrown shell of the grand house it once was. It had been abandoned and ready for demolition. Both my parents had passed by now. I was now the next generation. It was nostalgic, nonetheless. We reconnected with my sister, Scarlett, and other family and re-visited the places John and I spent our happy days in. It was shocking to see how unkind the years had been to Scarlett. I was much older than Scarlett, but the years and lifestyle had not been kind to her. Scarlett was crippled with arthritis and walked with a cane. Her beautiful legs were a memory, and her curly raven hair was thin and almost gone. I'm sure she wondered why she had turned her back on John in that dance hall that many years ago. Scarlett's life would have unfolded differently. She was still the light-hearted, happy soul I had left years ago, but nothing else was the same. Everything looked different. I suppose I was looking with different eyes. I thought about my beautiful, big house in the States with a pool, house at the beach, and cabin in the mountains, and how hard John worked to care for me and provide for his girls and get to the million-dollar goal. I felt blessed.

Nothing much had changed for Scarlett. She was a widow and still lived in that little bungalow alone. A visit to the dance hall was the same, but of course we were much older; we danced to the same music that is so timeless. The organ even still came up from the floor. It was like a picture of youth that fades from young to old. John and I danced for hours, pretending to recapture the energy that brought us together. It was magic. It was to be our last journey.

The last manor house where we stayed had large oil paintings on the wall that looked vaguely familiar. When my old uncle and aunt passed, one of the daughters moved in to the estate. She had two sons. The boys were unruly and allowed to dance on the grand piano and throw darts at the portraits in the parlor. When I got a closer look at the paintings in the manor house we were staying in, I could see tiny holes, dart holes. Perhaps in some quirky way, it was a sign my life was over and they were calling me home. I said nothing as I processed what I had seen, trying to make some sense out of something that made no sense.

When we returned home, we enjoyed watching the twins grow and change through the years. Jim lost his job at the bank, which put him in such a tailspin that he had a heart attack but he recovered. Jim was too old and had no education other than on-the-job training from the bank to get anything more than a menial job. To save face, John took Jim into the business with the idea that he was helping out, which gave him an income and he saved face. That didn't last long, and Jim bowed out. John was a self-made man, which meant he didn't always follow the rules. "Jack of all trades, master of none" described John. Get 'er done. This was the kingdom John built and John was the king.

In an effort to help out, John gave Faith a job in the business against the advice of Joy. What a fatal mistake. John then gave Don a job. Don was useless. He was on drugs, and he had no education, no initiative, and he was still looking at Faith to fix his life. When Don wasn't mowing grass, he was smoking it. Don had little respect for Faith even though she did what she thought was her best for Don. Fixing the life of a child just teaches them to be codependent and they don't have life skills. I had done the same for Faith. Even Don's friends would come to see Faith just to get a hug from her big breasts. Rather than interpreting it as rude and disrespectful, Don thought it was funny. One can only imagine the turn of events.

In an effort to teach good ethics and honesty, Don would wage trouble. If John came down too hard, it would go to Faith, who would in turn come to me to get to her John. If Don didn't want to come to work, it was okay; if

Don wanted to go to the beach, it was okay. If Don wanted to sleep in, it was okay. John had strong work ethic and believed in hard work. Hard work and Don were not in the same category. Oh, Don was front and center on payday. It was not okay. Poor John was always in time-out and he was only trying to help. The pressure cooker John found himself in would eventually take his life. They say God won't give you any more than you can handle, so I guess John couldn't take any more.

Although Faith and Don were working and taking paychecks, on John's last Thanksgiving he was rejected by the daughter he had accepted as his own. Joy had established a routine of going out of town to avoid the invitation to Thanksgiving dinner since the twins refused to go. John and I spent Thanksgiving alone. The pressure took a toll on me as well. I started to slip out of reality. On one particular dinner out with John, I thought I was on a date and told my husband of fifty-five years he couldn't come into the house. I was losing it. I started doing crazy stuff at the office, paying bills twice and some not at all, which was affecting the credit. I suppose it's the upside of memory loss; you establish your own world and step out of reality as reality bites.

One morning John rolled out of bed as usual but ended up on the floor. John was a big man, twice my size. I told John to get up and get in the car. I would take him to the hospital. I don't know why I didn't call 911. John was able to crawl to the car for the short drive to the hospital. It was too early to wake any of the family, so I took John to the hospital and dropped him off, and then I went home to wait for a decent hour to phone. I phoned Joy but she was at the gym. I told Hunter what had happened. Hunter came over and that was pretty much the beginning of the end for John.

Faith was hungry for money and knew where the pot of gold was. Faith and her son, Don, were relentless and took control of the situation. I was confused and went into a made-up dream world. I moved in with Joy and Hunter. I feared living in my big house alone. They were very kind. We were at the hospital every day. John suffered a heart attack, which affected the worst part of the heart. It was explained to us with pictures and x-rays. It was repeated a number of times that his age was a factor. They were pretty much writing him off. I remember hearing John say he didn't want to be seventy, so be careful what you wish for. John received poor treatment but went through the motions, caught in the medical wheel that seems to go 'round and 'round. John seemed to be improving, even joking with the nurses. John always had a good sense of humor and was well liked and respected with the exception of Faith, Jim, and Don. John was always the optimist. He seemed to be improving and ready to be moved to progressive care from the intensive care unit.

There was a line in the sand at this time between the two girls. It was all about opportunity, control, and power on one side and compassion and support on the other. I was caught in the middle in my dream world. We got a late-night call from the hospital to get there ASAP. You know as you walk down the hall late at night and see a chaplain coming the other direction, while it should give you comfort, it is not a good sign. John went code blue. That's fatal.

We formed a prayer circle. Faith would not come into the circle of life. Perhaps she never was. Guess she didn't belong there. Faith was an outsider; she was there alone. Jim and Don did not come with her to support her. After all, the man dying was not her father. How stupid could Faith be? There was no emotion or response to the gravity of the moment on her part.

We entered the room to see a nurse applying pressure to John's leg to keep the blood from flying out. John was struggling for his last breath. We didn't need to see the last breath to know it was coming. Joy stood over John with tears streaming and gave him permission to end his journey on earth with a promise she would watch over his English rose. With that permission, a tear rolled from his closed eyes. We returned home and within an hour got the call John was called home. John was sixty-nine, so he was granted his last wish not to be seventy. Perhaps it was a blessing since John was such a strong person; he would not have accepted the limitations of old age.

John had a good life with few issues until the end. He worked hard and achieved his million-dollar goal. I was angry John left me. I know there were probably warning signs of a heart condition John probably ignored. He was, after all, a hard-headed, tough German just like his mother. John worked hard and played hard. John completed sixty-nine years of good times, so how can you be sorry for the loss? John promised he would never leave me. Why didn't John take me with him?

None of us had much experience with this death business. I thought we had taken care of our final arrangements years ago, but it was not to be. John's body was transferred to a local funeral home and prepared for burial. We had purchased two plots years ago, but when I asked for a headstone I was told the rules had changed and I would have to use both plots for one stone. I was, however, able to trade those plots for a crypt. They happened to have one available on the top row. They said it was a good place since it was on the top, which is closer to heaven. It was a business putting dead people to rest, and they were making money at a time family was most vulnerable. So done deal, and there was room for me when the time came. The drawer holds two coffins. In my mind's eye, I thought John would love to be on top. John was always on top of the world.

There was no service or funeral. Joy made arrangements for the pastor of her church to come to the cemetery for a private service with family. Before that service took place, I asked Faith to see John one more time. I was denied. Faith offered to drop me off at the funeral home but would not go in. I needed to have Faith with me. I was always there for her. Why couldn't she be there for me? It was finished.

A week later, I received a call from the cemetery. There was a crypt available next to ours if I wanted to reserve and pay for it for family. I quickly acknowledged it and offered to purchase two, one for each of the girls. Joy accepted the gift but Faith said she preferred cremation. Hmm...makes sense.

Now dementia has an up side to it since you are living in a dream world. It's an out-of-body experience that shields and protects you from reality. That's where I was, stuck in my made-up dream world, at times back at the manor house sliding down the staircase with my cousins. All contact was severed at that point with the girls. I lived with one while the other was busy getting me to sign away everything she could get her hands on.

Within a week of the death, Faith put all of John's personal possessions on the street for trash. All traces of my beloved husband John were destroyed. Was this the way Faith had to deal with her past? Did she really resent everything John did for her? Was Faith angry about her life? Was Faith confused about her roots? Well, don't punish the child for the sins of the father or, in this case, the mother.

After several outings alone with Faith, it was revealed a number of documents had been signed, although I was cautioned not to sign anything without the advice of an attorney. Faith now had total control with a powerful document of power of attorney. When it was revealed I had signed the papers, I returned to my big house alone. Faith decided I should not be alone, as she was aware of my dementia, so she placed her son, Don, in the house. Don wasn't much help, as he came in late, went to bed, locked the door, and left the next day. I was still driving and got lost most of the times. I lost my way as my mind was beginning to get lost. One time I drove and drove, trying to find my way home. Just as I was about to run out of gas, I found my house. Scared, I promised myself I would not do that again.

It was agreed I should move into a progressive-care facility. It was a beautiful retirement community. I thought I was living in a five-star hotel. Oh, how proud my mother would be. I had many friends, activities, and a support group. I was truly happy. Friday dinners with Joy continued, and Joy made sure I got to church as usual on Sunday mornings. Life was good again. I had a lovely apartment with all my things. I began to wander the halls, not knowing day from night.

One night I prepared drinks for the men who were in the basement working, only to realize there were no men and no basement. One night I was found walking down the middle of a busy road at 2:00 A.M. I was fortunate to have been found and returned. Before my big house was sold, I would leave my apartment and drive back to the house and fall asleep in the only thing left in the house, a well-used recliner John had spent many hours in the last of his days. I could smell his odor and feel his touch. I felt his presence in that chair and reassurance he would take care of his English rose. Thank goodness I stopped driving before the house was sold and I could no longer make the trip back to the chair. I could very well have been a frequent visitor to a new family—a ghost from the past of that house, a ghost with a heartbeat.

My physical appearance began to change as my health went into a downward spiral. The staff from the retirement center made contact with Faith, as she had the POA, and suggested I go to the next level of care in assisted living. Faith was enraged and determined I was not to go there, although I was eval-

uated and determined for my safety it was what needed to happen. It is a rec-
ommendation from the retirement facility for the good. There are three levels
of care, and this was the next phase. Faith didn't want to face the reality of my
decline.

Joy and Hunter picked me up as usual for a Friday night dinner. I was to
go to a festival with them the next day, which was also the twins' birthday.
When they dropped me off, Faith was lurking in the dark, waiting for my
return. When I got to my apartment, Faith came up and explained I was to be
moved to assisted living and that was not happening. I think Faith thought she
was losing more control and wanted to hide me away until she could finish
gathering all the assets together. Anyway, Faith said she had found a nice lady
in a nice home to care for me. I was in no position to fight the situation and
trusted Faith.

Faith packed my bags, and off we went in the dead of night. I was afraid.
I could feel the anger from Faith and wanted to call Joy and Hunter. Where
was I going and why? I didn't understand. As night falls, an innocent mother
calls for her daughter. It wasn't to be. The front desk was informed as we
walked away that no one was putting her mother away.

We drove to a home and were met by a well-dressed but obese black lady
and her husband. Why would Faith do this to me? The black lady escorted me
to a bedroom with my suitcase. This was where I was to live the rest of my
days. I was told to have nothing to do with Joy, and if I were to be confronted
I was to runaway. When Joy came to pick me up for the festival the next day,
she found out I was MIA. Joy was told I left in the night with Faith and they
didn't know where I went. Joy went to the home of Faith and was promptly
rejected. Faith and Jim wouldn't open the door and spoke through the closed
door; they said they couldn't help her and she should go away.

I had been thrust into an abyss. The black lady prepared food I didn't
know and forced me to eat it. I needed a cup of tea. Tea always makes you feel
better. I was denied. They took me to an all-black church, and the lady insisted
on bathing me and violating my privacy. I was nothing. Oh, the dark journey
I was taking again. This time, however, I could slip into my dream world and
all the deposits I had in my memory bank. It was my escape from the hell
Faith put me in. How could the very child I would lay my life down for put
me in this place with these people? Was this my fate for sin?

Hunter followed Faith to the place I had been put. There was a knock at
the door, but the lady said she was employed by Faith and answered only to
her. Joy was at the door, pleading and crying, but it was to no avail; she was
there to rescue me and yet I was weak and afraid. Joy left time after time, rejected, feeling deserted and alone. How could I as a mother reject her child,
my Joy? Where was John? Why would John not come for me? It was the first
time I had missed the twins' birthday, and it made me sad.

I was forced to sign a document stating I never wanted to see Joy or my
granddaughters again. That was far from the truth; they were my happy place.
It was very painful for me to read a lie, but I had no choice but to sign it. As

a last resort, Joy went to seek legal advice and file papers for guardianship. Faith had a counter suit filed and the whole mess ended up in court. The attorneys were a sharp contrast. The only attorney Faith could find was from a large high-priced firm. The attorney couldn't even pronounce her name. Joy's attorney had been around a long time. He looked like Jimmy Cagney and took his cases to heart. He spent hours pouring over case law and was even asked to leave the library as they were closing because he was researching and preparing for the court date. He had a strong accounting background, he was an honest lawyer, which was a bonus, and he was lectured on guardianships. He took on cases with passion and only accepted a case if he believed a wrong had to be righted. Joy was confident she had made the right selection and decision.

Faith thought she would win the case, but there were no winners in this battle. I had been evaluated by numerous physicians and declared incompetent. John worked hard all his life and was always looking to save a dollar. John's attorney was sleazy, the accountant incompetent, and financial advisor controlling. John's attorney represented me at the hearing, but there was little he could do with all the documentation and girls fighting for control. Faith had lots of players in her corner and believed she would win the case. The missing link for Faith was the truth. A truth will always surface somewhere along the way.

It was a nasty fight, ultimately ending in the court appointing a legal guardian. Joy's attorney was brilliant and his performance in front of the judge worthy of an Academy Award. At least it stopped the money flow and ended the control Faith had or thought she had.

Joy was granted visitation rights and picked me up from the black family for outings. The happy times always ended with tears from Joy and myself. I didn't want to go back into that house, and Joy didn't want me to go back. I was trapped in a strange house with strange things happening in my head. Before the guardianship was granted, the black lady took advantage of me and used my credit card to provide a nice Christmas for her family. The black lady told the guardian I needed my teeth whitened, and of course, she had hers whitened along with me. How could Faith allow that to happen?

Joy picked me up one last time from the black lady and was taken aback as I stood at the front door with snow-white teeth, a long blonde wig, and fur coat that went to the ground. I was a virtual freak show, certainly not the proper English rose I once was. I always prided myself in looking my best.

I went to another facility when the black lady washed her hands of it. She didn't like Joy and Joy didn't like her or the situation and control she had. I finally left but not until after I was raped by the husband. I was weak and could not fight back. I slipped back into a dreamlike state and pretended it was John. Everything looks the same in the dark. It was so real to me that when I eventually returned to the assisted care level of the very facility I was kidnapped from, I actually went through the birthing process. Joy was mortified when the staff told her about the incident but had no proof and knew in her heart I was safe at last.

Faith took over the business she got in the settlement, writing out a big paycheck for her son, Don. Faith borrowed a lot of money from the bank as the building was paid. She was left with a big attorney bill and an environmental clean-up from some of the chemicals that had been dumped in the ground. The loan officer was actually an old colleague of her husband, Jim, from his banking days, and although it was a poor decision he slipped the note through the system. It didn't last long, and the business went into default and Faith walked away. All the years of blood, sweat, and tears were gone. Oh, John met his million-dollar goal, but there was little left when Faith finished. At least the actions taken by Joy were in time to save enough for me to finish my earthly journey.

I went back to the very place I was taken from and was quite happy with all the activities. I got to go to church again with Joy and her husband, and Friday night dinners resumed. I was able to attend the weddings of the twins. The first wedding Faith showed up uninvited and was not happy when she was denied sitting with the family. Perhaps I had dropped Faith on her head at some time. I wonder what she was thinking. It was a steady and slow decline, and I died one drop at a time. I guess it was my punishment for my sins of the past.

The guardian was now taking money and could pretty much call the shots. She requested and received an additional $10,000 a month she said was needed for my care. She became a good friend to Faith, and Joy was out of the loop. I was victimized again. They determined that although the facility I was in provided the best care, I should have twenty-four-hour private duty care in addition. That care consisted of black or Spanish staff watching the TV they wanted to watch, sleeping in a chair, or talking on the phone. They helped with meals, but the facility had staff to do that. I was bedridden in the end, so why did I need twenty-four-hour care?

The money was flying. I prayed I would not outlive my money. My God, why have you forsaken me? A journey is a walk in faith. I remembered footsteps and knew I was not alone. Stop, look, and listen; the Prince of Peace lives in your heart, the path is clear, and signs are there to guide you. You are never alone. If you believe, you will find your way to the Kingdom.

I soon slipped into the next phase and was transferred to skilled nursing. I had a number of small strokes, which took a little more of me with each episode. I lost control of my bladder and had to wear diapers. Faith came on a daily basis and changed my diaper. Perhaps Faith thought that act of kindness would fix all the wrong she had done. Old once and young twice, I suppose. I started to lose weight and forgot how to swallow. I did live long enough for Joy to release me from my guilt as she asked the tough question, Do Faith and I have different fathers? I was unable to speak, but I was able to weep and nod my head. What a revelation and release. The eyes are the window to the soul. My Joy had her father's eyes. I thought, *Keep moving through the sea of life, my child; there will be times of calm before the storm.*

Sometimes rip currents will seem to take you away, but remember always to swim parallel and you will find your way back.

Why did I keep the secret all those years? I felt the peace that passes all understanding clothe me and I could finish my journey on earth and move to the next level. The truth will set you free. I hope someday at some place Faith will find that peace and forgiveness. I will be in one of my Father's mansions, continuing to shield, protect, and look after my children.

The angels finally closed my eyes. I ran into the light faster and faster, and I'm restored and whole and free—free at last to be me and be reunited once again with John. I can see clearly now, the rain is gone. I know there is no mansion in my Father's house for Faith as she drifts "Out to See." I was there to hear her borning cry, and I'll be there until her journey ends.

CPSIA information can be obtained at www.ICGtesting.com
Printed in the USA
LVOW010054141212

311597LV00013B/247/P